Achieving Mediocrity

Surefire Strategies for a Lackluster Life

By Valentine J. Brkich

Copyright © 2014 Valentine J. Brkich

First published in the United States in 2014.

Published by Bridge Street Books (Beaver, Pa.)

ISBN 978-0-9816877-7-3

Cover design by Brkich Design (brkichdesign.com)

Photography by Alessa Yanssens (rsvpink.com)

To my wife, for marrying a hopeless dreamer and for sticking by me through it all.

(Don't worry, hon. I'll figure it all out soon.)

(Maybe.)

Introduction

It seems nowadays like everyone has a book on helping people find success. Just search "success" on Amazon.com and you'll get roughly 186,864 results. Happiness is another popular subject, with 38,896 titles currently available. That's a lot of competition.

But if you search for books on "mediocrity," you know how many results pop up? 357. That's one of the reasons I decided to write this: there's a clear market for books on how to be just average. And since they always say "write what you know," it seemed like a no-brainer. After all, I'm an expert on the subject.

After a promising youth where my potential seemed unlimited, my post-collegiate working years have been, for want of a better word, lackluster. I ended up bouncing around from job to job – 15 in all! – until the birth of my children forced me to hunker down and take a normal, dependable, desk job. (Thanks a lot, kids.) Now, here I am in my 40s, and there's little chance I'm ever going to accomplish my childhood dream of becoming an astronaut. Or Indiana Jones. Or starting QB for the Pittsburgh Steelers. Instead, I'm just another working schlep, as they say.

How did I achieve this life of astonishing level of mediocrity, you ask? Well, it took a lot of hard work and determination. Actually, scratch that. It was simple: I just screwed around a lot and didn't really put much thought into my future. In hindsight, I guess it wasn't the best plan.

Then again, who's to say what truly defines success? Sure, society would like you to believe that success is all about making a ton of cash and living in some palatial estate in Malibu. But like a wise man (Biggie Smalls) once said, "Mo money, mo problems." Amen.

This book is for those of you who don't really give a hoot about success and all the burdens that come along with it. It's for people who are completely content with living a normal, boring, middle-class lifestyle and working at some mundane, unexceptional job with little or no impact on society.

Sure, I could've written yet another motivational book about how to find success and happiness and fulfillment in your life. But that's been done to death. Besides, such a project would require a positive attitude and a strong work ethic. Neither of which are really my thing.

Each chapter offers a new rule for NOT finding success in your life. If you follow these rules, I assure you that your life will turn out just as mediocre and unfulfilling as mine—maybe even less!

So without further ado…prepare to be underwhelmed!

RULE #1: Ignore Your Natural Talents

I always knew I was going to be a writer.

Actually, at first I was pretty sure I was going to be an astronaut. Either that or Indiana Jones. Then the Challenger exploded. Cross out astronaut. Then I learned that archaeology wasn't as glamorous as it appeared in the movies, and that it rarely involved navigating booby-trapped South American tombs or fighting Nazis. Which to me were the only reasons to get into the field in the first place. So I scratched that one from the list, too.

But I always loved telling stories. And besides, I could always *write* about exploring space or discovering hidden treasure. Or fighting Nazis. So that's just what I did. I filled notebook after notebook with my tales of adventure, which I wrote mostly during class when the teacher wasn't looking. Over the years I honed my craft, and soon my writing ability was being noticed in my schoolwork as well. All I had to do was keep up with it and a career as a successful writer was all but guaranteed!

But then I just stopped writing.

Oh, sure, I wrote for my classes whenever the assignment called for it. But as for writing simply for the pure enjoyment of it, I quit as soon as I entered high school. I'm not sure why, exactly. Maybe I couldn't think of anymore stories about sea monsters or space battles or rugged adventurers named Dakota Smith who were obvious rip-offs of Indiana Jones (a purely hypothetical example, of course). Plus, I had more important things to study, like chemistry, trigonometry, and humanities—you know, practical subjects the public education system decided would be of value to me down the road in my career as a scientist/mathematician by day, art critic/philosopher by night.

I didn't start writing for pleasure again until well after college, when I was trapped in boring dead-end job after boring dead-end job, and I needed something to do to pass the time between making copies and distributing the mail. (*Mediocrity Secret: Only apply to dead-end jobs with little or no chance for advancement!*) By then I'd lost most of the natural creativity and imagination that had made me such a good writer in the first place. My muse had been muted by the tedium of everyday office life.

All through high school, I could have been building upon my natural talents by writing every day, seeking out writing mentors, attending writing conferences and actively participating in writing groups. Of course, all of this is crystal clear in hindsight. But back then my brain had been hijacked by my hormones, which could care less about my God-given abilities and were only concerned with one thing: girls. And try as you might, you just can't fight the life force.

So if you want to find yourself trapped in some unsatisfying job that has you questioning the meaning of life day after dreary day – and who doesn't? – be sure to ignore your natural abilities and let them wither away. In no time you'll find yourself stuck in a nice, cushy, boring-as-hell office job!

Otherwise you might turn out to be successful *and* happy. But that's a whole 'nother book altogether.

RULE #2: Spend Your Time Screwing Off

One thing that successful people have in common is they use their time wisely. They take advantage of their downtime to further educate themselves on things they're passionate about. They find resources for honing their skills. They get involved with clubs and groups and organizations that enable them to meet new people and build valuable relationships with others.

Sounds exhausting, right?

Throughout my teens and twenties, when I wasn't in class or at work, I was basically doing nothing. And loving every minute of it.

In high school I had one priority: find beer. I take that back. I had TWO priorities: 1) find beer, 2) find girls. (Not necessarily in that order.) My friends and I would steal from my dad's stash of Old Milwaukee and then go out into the woods to suck down the lukewarm liquid. We weren't picky. Then we'd go off in search of the elusive female, which to us was like trying to locate Bigfoot.

Other times, i.e., every weekend, we'd track down an of-legal-age friend to make a beer run for us. After that we'd head to the mall, where we'd do laps around the place looking for the hottest girls we could find and then do absolutely nothing about it. Then we'd go off into the woods again to drink our beer. Alone.

When I was 17 I paid a kid $20 for a fake I.D. so I wouldn't have to depend on theft or the kindness of certain elders in order to acquire my beloved malted beverage. After standing in the long line that stretched outside of the counterfeiter's house, I made it inside where a huge cardboard cutout of a South Carolina I.D. hung on the wall. I stepped in front of the little blue square, tried my best to look twenty-something, and then two weeks later my very own laminated fake driver's license was hand-delivered to me at my locker between Spanish and biology. From then on by day I was Val Brkich, but by night I was William Bailey (*Axl Rose's real name*), of Charleston, South Carolina, age 25.

The fake I.D. worked like a charm. For a while. I was careful at first, only going to a local dive bar to buy 40s every now and then. But then I got greedy, and it got taken from me at a beer distributor my freshman year of college during a road trip to Erie. I guess the store's owner didn't buy my fake southern drawl. Or that I was 25 when I actually looked 14.

Instead of always running around looking for my next buzz or another girl I was never going to talk to, I could've been doing something more productive, like writing. Then again, my beer tolerance level would have been embarrassingly low by the time I reached college.

Meanwhile, while I was out on my never-ending quest for beer and girls, the people I know now who are successful were the ones at home studying or at play practice or at their Junior Achievement meetings, using (rather than killing) their brain cells and making authentic connections with other people that would help them down the road in their career.

Suckers!

Sure, maybe they're enjoying the fruits of their labor now, doing fulfilling work and living the life they always dreamed of. But I bet none of them ever experienced the thrill of chugging a warm Old Mil out behind their parents' shed.

And those types of memories are priceless.

RULE #3: Don't Get Involved

You know who I could never understand back in high school? Those kids who got involved in every club and group available to them, effectively limiting their free time and preventing them from doing something worthwhile like playing video games, hanging out at the mall, or drinking lukewarm beer in the woods.

Some people just don't get it.

Take the kids in the band, for example. I still see them out there every year in early August, long before the school year starts, practicing their songs and formations at some ungodly hour. Why would anyone actually choose to do that? While they were up at the crack of dawn marching around the parking lot, I was all nice and cozy at home in my bed. And when they were back out there again in the evening, I'd was out with my friends roaming the mall in search of girls we'd never get up the nerve to talk to.

Again, kids, it's all about priorities.

I actually knew some kids who were in the band *and* the school play *and* who were also members of student council, Spanish Club, the yearbook staff, National Honor Society, Glee Club, and so on. Not me. While they were waking up before sunrise for band practice, I was chilling out on my couch watching old re-runs of "The Three Stooges." While they were stuck inside rehearsing for the high school musical, I was out honing my skateboarding skills. While they were staying after school for Debate Club, I was out playing wiffle ball in the park.

I think it's clear who was using their time more wisely.

Sure, maybe being involved in so many different things helped them to develop their social skills and learn how to deal with different types of people. Maybe they learned how to be organized and on time and how to multi-task. And maybe doing things like band and the play taught them the value of hard work and how good it feels to dedicate yourself to something and then see it come to fruition after hours and hours of practice. They probably even made some deep, long-lasting relationships that continue to this day and that have helped them become successful in whatever it is they do.

Big whoop. While they were busy overachieving, I was off having a great time with my friends and building memories that would last a lifetime. Like that time I sang karaoke at the mall, and that hot girl said I had a good voice. (At least that's what she told my friend's friend's friend.) Sure, maybe nothing ever came out of it. But it could have. Probably. And there were a bunch of other memorable times like that too. I just can't remember any of them right now.

I'll admit it, most of the kids I knew in high school who got involved in a lot of groups and activities are now doing well in rewarding careers that they enjoy. But that's probably just a coincidence.

Besides, how many of them ever rocked "Dust in the Wind" at their local mall?

I rest my case.

RULE #4: Never Give 100 Percent

You see it time and time again. The most successful people in the world are the ones who work the hardest; the ones who put in the time and give it everything they have. Big mistake.

It's hard work being successful. You have to be dedicated and passionate. You have to stay up late studying. You have to stay after practice and keep practicing long after everyone else has gone home for dinner. You have to make an effort to reach out to people you admire and ask for their advice and guidance. Makes me tired just thinking about it.

On the other hand, if you're a "half-asser" (as my wife calls me), you can easily coast your way to a relaxing life of mediocrity by making sure that you never give 100 percent in anything you do.

For example, I started playing soccer at the age of 6 and continued playing up until my senior year in high school, when I quit the team because I wasn't playing enough. As a result I didn't get to experience senior night. (*Mediocrity Secret: A sure way to ward off success is to quit whenever things aren't going your way!)* At the time I blamed my coach. But the truth is he didn't play me because I wasn't very good. I could have been, that is, if I had put in any extra effort at all and practiced more than just what was mandated by the team.

But then again I would've let down the guys down at the wiffle ball game.

After I quit soccer, a friend convinced me to join the track team. I had always been a fast runner, so it seemed like a good fit. Too bad nobody told me how hard track was. I mean, you had to run. Like every day! And during the meets sometimes you actually had to run more than one race—three or four in my case. It was stressful. So much so that every once in a while my friend and I would go behind the bleachers for a smoke between races, just to calm our nerves.

Truth be told I did pretty well in track despite my lackluster effort. I never came in first, but I came in second all the time, which is just as good. Well, almost.

What I'm trying to say is, unless you're Lebron James and you hit the genetic lottery, you're going to have to work hard and really give it your all in order to excel in anything, sports or otherwise.

However, if you're OK with living a so-so life, just remember the Mediocrity Maxim: Good enough is good enough.

It's got me where I am today. And it can do the same for you!

RULE #5: Wait Until College to Figure It All Out

Mediocrity isn't just something that falls into your lap. In order to be a true underachiever, you have to make a deliberate, conscious decision to be indecisive in just about every aspect of your life. One such example is failing to decide until *after* you graduate high school what you plan to do with your life.

As I mentioned before, at an early age I discovered my proclivity for writing, a talent which, if I had taken it seriously, could have been developed and sharpened over the course of my adolescent years and given me a clear direction for study as I headed into higher education. But since I had abandoned this natural skill early on in order to pursue my other passions – beer and girls – by the time I was ready to graduate high school I had absolutely no idea what to study in college.

Heck, I hadn't even looked into any colleges. The only one I visited was the one I ended up attending, and that was only because my older sister already went there, and she took me to a frat party during my one and only visit. I was sold after I saw the first keg. Plus, the school had a 4-to-1 girl-to-guy ratio. I couldn't sign up fast enough.

So when it came time to decide on my life's pursuit, I picked something that sounded good: computers. I mean, who doesn't like computers, right? They're everywhere! Talk about job security. Besides, my sister was studying computers and she liked it. And my dad was a computer programmer with a good-paying gig downtown. I was going to be a computer programmer! Done and done.

Of course, what they don't tell you is that computers are complicated beasts that operate via some bizarre system revolving around ones and zeros. And the so-called "languages" they tried to get me to learn were more incomprehensible than the Spanish I had studied for three years and still couldn't speak. If there was any chance I was going to figure out any of this computer stuff, I was actually going to have to study, and not just at nighttime—on the weekends, too! Good luck with that. I was paying good money to go to college (actually, my dad was), and I wasn't about to miss out on all the parties, video game marathons, and afternoon keggers.

After all, isn't that what college is all about?

Eventually I switched to a different major that didn't require as much of my valuable free time: English Lit. As a result, I graduated with flying colors and a degree that would have me hopping cluelessly from job to job over the next decade.

But in my four years of college I can say that I rarely missed a party.

And that should be worth something. Right?

RULE #6: Education Schmeducation

College is expensive. That's why my parents were thrilled when I was awarded my school's Trustee's Scholarship, which paid for half of my tuition. That is, as long as I kept up my grades. Which, of course, I did not.

The deal was, during my first year of college I had to maintain a 3.30 GPA. It should've been no big deal, since I'd always been an A student. The thing is, nobody told me there'd be so much beer in college. I'm talking tons. Come to think of it, yes they did. It's one of the main reasons I couldn't wait to get started.

After my first year, in order to keep my scholarship, all I had to do was maintain a solid 3.00 for the remainder of my college career. Piece of cake. Heck, I'd graduated high school with a 3.30 GPA without hardly ever studying at all. I could maintain a B average in my sleep.

The thing is, it's hard to keep up a steady partying schedule while taking advanced math classes and learning how to become a computer programmer. These things just don't mesh.

Plus, now that I was on my own it was up to me to be a responsible young man and make the right decisions. I was an adult, after all. (At least according to the federal government.) So I had to make a choice: either cut back on partying, hunker down and focus on my academics, or party like a rock star and risk it all.

Quiz time! Which option do you think I chose? (*Hint: There's no beer in Intro to COBOL.*)

I ended up losing my prestigious scholarship after just one semester. That was a fun phone call home. And by the end of the first semester of my sophomore year my GPA had plummeted to an all-time low of 2.60, and I was a terrible programmer to boot. Personally, I blame it on my computer professors, who seemed more machine than man and had a difficult time explaining things to a normal, English-speaking human such as myself. Then again it may have had something to do with the fact that I dedicated more time to working on my beer-pong skills than to my coding homework. Maybe I couldn't tell an algorithm from Al Gore, but I could sink a back-corner Solo cup like nobody's business!

And in life, it's the practical skills that truly matter.

Eventually my father had enough of my partying ways and threatened to enlist me in the Army unless I got my act together. Over break we had an actual sit-down discussion about it – with the TV off! – so I knew he was serious.

So when I went back to school I decided to make a drastic change about my college career, and I switched my major from computers to the up-and-coming field of English Literature! I'm not sure it's what my dad had in mind, but I was able to turn my grades around make the Dean's List every semester from there on out. And I avoided being forced into military service.

So, kids, the real lesson here is: When the going gets tough, always look for the easy way out. The path of least resistance is a well-trodden path for good reason.

RULE #7: Whenever Possible, Procrastinate

During the latter half of my college career I was able to turn my academic standing around and finish with flying colors, whatever the hell that means. Sure, maybe I had no idea what I was going to do with a degree in English Lit, but I wasn't worried. My guidance counselor had assured me that English majors "could do anything!" He even showed me a long list of English alums who had gone on to work in a variety of fields.

Years later I discovered the reason for this occupational diversity is because English majors pretty much *have* to be flexible when it comes to work. Apparently there isn't a big demand out there for people who can compare and contrast the Romantic poets.

As my final year in college dwindled away, I started to think maybe I should consider getting an internship to see what life was like in the real world. I knew a lot of other kids who began interning during their junior year, which wasn't very smart, if you ask me. While they were off sneaking a peek at the future, I was focusing on the present, i.e., honing my beer-pong skills and becoming a dedicated member of Tequila Club.

Point: me.

January of my senior year I landed an internship with the *In Pittsburgh Newsweekly,* an arts-and-entertainment publication based in the city's super-hip South Side neighborhood. Each day that month I rode the bus downtown to my temporary job, where I learned the ins and outs of the publishing biz. Actually I just "designed" classified ads in Microsoft Word and tried to look busy the rest of the time (a useful skill I'd use in just about every job from there on out).

I did learn something very valuable through that experience, though. I learned that I really, really wanted to go back to school and never, ever go back to the so-called real world again. (*Mediocrity Secret: Put off the "real-world" as long as possible!*)

When I finally returned to school in February, I was in heaven. I felt like George Bailey in *It's A Wonderful Life* —I had gotten to see what life was like after college, and it wasn't pretty. From that moment on I wasn't going to take a minute of my college experience for granted. By the end of the year, not only was I a beer-pong ace, but I had also been promoted to President of Tequila Club. All it took was a little hard work and dedication.

So I guess I was wrong about RULE #4. If you give something your all, you really can accomplish great things. Take this ebook, for example. I've been thinking about writing it for years. But I just kept putting it off and putting it off, mainly because I was busy working on breaking my personal record for computer Solitaire (30 seconds!). If I would've shown some ambition and written it earlier, I wouldn't have had all the mediocrity cred that I do now, which, inevitably, would've hurt my book's sales.

So you see, kids, it's all about the journey. You may feel lost. You may think you're trapped in a hopeless situation with no way out. But if you're patient (i.e., if you embrace procrastination) and you don't stress too much about all the ups and downs along the way, it may only take you 17 or 18 years to come to terms with your mediocrity.

And I'm living proof.

RULE #8: Veg-Out in Front of the Tube

After graduating with a degree in English Lit, my mind was chock full of knowledge about some of history's greatest writers, not to mention a good amount of tequila residue. But before diving head first into the rat race, I decided to take a little time off before beginning the next phase of my life. I had put in four long years of partying, chasing girls, and, yes, some studying. Now it was my chance to sit back on the couch and reflect on those years while devouring Oreos and watching "The Price is Right." After all, I had earned it.

So for the next three months or so, I took it easy and enjoyed what would be the last free summer of my life. I woke up late, hung out in my PJs, and caught up on some quality daytime television—something I had been deprived of over the past four years due to being stuck in class. I had the rest of my life to worry about jobs and money and making something of myself. This was my time to shine! And by that I mean doing as little as possible.

Of course I couldn't avail my parents of my less-than-ambitious plan for summer sloth. So every morning while sipping my coffee and inhaling Double-Stufs, I perused the classifieds to make it seem like I was actually making a concerted effort to do something with my life. Little did they know that I was actually just watching Plinko.

You know what's funny? Three months isn't as long as it seems. (Apparently it's just 90 days or so.) Before I knew it, August was upon me and it was time for me to enter the workforce. Luckily I was pretty much Showcase-Showdowned out by then.

Surprisingly, though, the workforce wasn't in dire need of someone who could comment on the symbolism in *Moby Dick*. This of course was back during the great Literature Recession of 1997.

It was at this time when I started to question the wisdom of switching majors from computers to English Lit. Sure, it seemed like the right decision at the time, but so did splitting a bottle of Cuervo between four people. In hindsight my judgment may have been somewhat impaired.

So, desperately in need of some cash and ravaged with sofa sores, I took the first job I could find: stock boy at a local office supply store. Not exactly the dream job I'd hoped for after earning my degree (i.e., Toy Player-Wither, a la Tom Hank's character in the movie "Big"). But it would have to do for now.

Besides, you can't start at the top. Right? Hopefully, with a little hustle and determination, I'd work my way up to bigger and better things, like cashier or – dare to dream – assistant manager. Anything was possible! *(Spoiler Alert: I quit three weeks later.)*

RULE #9: Work a Bunch of Crappy Jobs and Do Nothing to Try to Improve Yourself

Success comes from having a clear idea of where you want to go, putting in the hard work, and then moving from one step to the next until you achieve your goal.

Mediocrity, on the other hand, is usually the result of a pattern of indecisiveness, innate inadequacy, and a shameful lack of ambition. This is the path I decided to take—and it's made all the difference!

If you really want to have a lackluster life and career, I recommend bouncing from one crappy job to the next without any purpose or direction. And while you're trapped in this merry-go-round of mediocrity, do absolutely nothing to improve your situation. Do not look into continuing your education. Do not reach out to those you admire for advice and guidance. And whatever you do, never ever sacrifice your precious free time in order to stop your downward spiral.

Otherwise you might just make something of yourself.

As I mentioned earlier, my first job out of college was as a stock boy for a major office supplies chain. I marched in three months after graduation, diploma in hand, and began my life's work: straightening three-ring binders on the shelf and making sure the pens-and-pencils aisle was nice and neat. But despite how rewarding that job was, I quickly grew tired of it and started off on an unprecedented, 15-year job-hopping journey, the likes of which had never been seen before:

- Stock boy at an office supply store
- Storm door "expert" at a home improvement store
- Appraisal admin for a title management company
- Data entry technician for a cable company
- Order entry specialist at a metal parts manufacturer
- Busboy at a popular theme restaurant (think "flair")
- Outside sales rep for a marketing company (3 whole days!)
- Administrative assistant at a major chemicals manufacturer
- Copywriter for a country radio conglomerate (Ugh)
- Administrative assistant for an insurance company (Double ugh)
- Sales and pricing coordinator back at the same chemicals manufacturer
- Inside sales rep for a company that made fireproof brick to line the interior of cement kilns (And, no, I'm not joking.)
- PR writer for a local hospital
- Freelance writer
- PR and marketing writer for a private university
- Freelance writer

Just think, if you do little or nothing to prepare for your career, and if you continue to do little or nothing until after you graduate, with a degree that you have no idea what to do with, you too could have an identical record of inadequacy.

Believe in yourself—you can do it!

But wait a second, you say, I thought you said this book is about mediocrity? It looks like you worked your way up and eventually built a pretty successful writing career. How is that mediocre?

True, Dear Reader. I can see your point. (And by "your point" I mean the imaginary point I imagined on your behalf.) My career path may have been somewhat circuitous, but I did end up doing work that I'm good at and that I truly enjoy. Some people might actually consider that as being successful.

But don't forget, originally I had plans to explore the galaxy and/or win the Super Bowl. So when you look at it that way, I'm as mediocre as they come.

RULE #10: Do Nothing and Just Hope for Things to Change on Their Own

Call me a dreamer, arrogant, or just downright delusional, but I've always felt I was meant for greatness. I was sure that one day when I grew up something really big would happen, and after that my life would be one exciting day after another as people showered me with money and gifts and praise for doing that really great thing. Whatever it was.

Well, I'm all grown up now. And…I'm still waiting.

As we covered earlier, at first I thought I'd go on to be a famous astronaut. I was certain of it, especially after the local AM radio station came to our school and asked me – on air! – what I wanted to be when I grew up, and emphatically I said "astronaut." There was no turning back after that. Not after blasting it out over the airwaves for everyone to hear. And by "everyone" I mean all the senior citizens within a couple miles or so. But then I realized you could actually be killed doing the astronaut thing, which greatly dampened my enthusiasm for the vocation.

But I wasn't worried. I was certain that something else would come to mind.

And it did. Not long after abandoning my orbital aspirations, I decided to be the next great quarterback for the Pittsburgh Steelers. It didn't matter that I had no experience playing actual football, or that I weighed 85 pounds soaking wet. Those were just minor obstacles. And even though I had no plans to actually join a team or attempt to get in football-playing shape, the way I saw it, if it was meant to be – and it certainly was – things would just work out on their own.

After all, from the time I was very young people had always told me I was destined for "big things." I even remember my best friend's mother stating that, and I quote, I would "probably end up being President of the United States someday." To tell you the truth, I wasn't sure if I really wanted the job, but it was nice knowing I had that to fall back on.

By now you've probably figured out that I never ended up becoming President. Turns out that, in addition to knowing something about politics and the government, you actually have to apply, or "run" as they call it, to even be considered for the position. Honestly, I'm amazed they're able to find interested candidates every four years.

I still have hope that something extraordinary will happen, though. What, I'm not sure? But I'll still continue to hope. And as a wise man once said, "Hope is a good thing, maybe the best of things, and no good thing ever dies."

OK, maybe Andy Dufresne isn't really a *real* person. Minor detail. But he's right, you know. At least about the hope stuff. Hope really is a good thing.

Good things, on the other hand, die all the time. So I'm not really sure where he was going with that.

Conclusion

Depressed? Good. You should be after reading that miserable chronicle of mediocrity. Heck, it's my story and even I feel a little down.

Hopefully you've figured out that this book isn't meant to be taken seriously. No one in their right mind would tell you to ignore your natural talents or to waste your education or to just hope that things will work out on their own. That's insane. Trust me. I know from experience.

I wrote this sad little tome so that young people could learn from my mistakes. I wrote it to save them from wasting their precious time and to help them start focusing on making their life what they always wanted it to be. I wrote it so that they wouldn't find themselves pushing 40 and still unsure of what they wanted to be when they grew up.

Not that I know anything about that.

Do I think every high school or college kid that reads this book will suddenly wake up and start taking his or her life seriously? Of course not. I was a kid once. I know how it works. I understand how they see us adults as "out-of-touch" and "preachy" and "old" and "out-of-shape" and "boring" and "unattractive" and "all up in their business," etc.

But that's OK. One day other kids will say the same thing about them. Which makes me very happy to think about.

If I can just save one young person, however, from wasting his or her formative years guzzling beer, screwing off, and not putting an ounce of thought or effort into the future, then it was worth the hours and hours – sad, isn't it? – that I spent at my computer recalling the many, many, many mistakes I've made thus far in my life.

It's simple: just do the exact opposite of everything you've read in this book and I guarantee that you'll be successful.

This is the point in the book where I'd usually invite the reader to feel free to reach out to me for advice or guidance. But considering what I've revealed in the previous pages, I seriously doubt anyone would take me up on the offer.

Good luck!

About the Author

Valentine J. Brkich is a writer, husband, and father (not necessarily in that order).

Visit him online at valentinebrkich.com.

Follow him on Twitter and Instagram at @valentinebrkich.

www.ingramcontent.com/pod-product-compliance
Lightning Source LLC
Chambersburg PA
CBHW020439030426
42337CB00014B/1328